# IS-922: Applications of GIS for Emergency Management

## By

## Fema

10/31/2013

# Lesson 1: Introduction and Course Overview

## Course Welcome

Welcome to the introduction to Applications of GIS for Emergency Management.

This course describes how Geographic Information Systems (GIS) work and how using GIS can improve emergency management.

## Applications of Geographic Information Systems (GIS) for Emergency Management

A Geographic Information System (GIS) is a database system with software that can analyze and display data, in a visual environment, using digitized maps and tables for planning and decisionmaking.

Maps and data may be layered, displayed, edited, and analyzed in literally thousands of different ways by careful selection of data-points being considered by the user.

GIS is a very useful tool for many aspects of emergency management including emergency response, planning, mitigation, exercises, homeland security, planning, response, and recovery.

GIS has robust modeling capabilities, allowing its users to adjust data and scenarios for prediction, planning, and estimation.

GIS capability is enhanced when FEMA's Hazus software and other tools are incorporated.

GIS provides emergency management personnel and decisionmakers the information they need to make accurate and timely decisions.

This course will introduce you to GIS and the value of using GIS in emergency management.

# Course Goal and Content

The goal of this course is to explore how GIS technology can support the emergency management community.

The topics addressed in this course include:

- GIS fundamentals and history.
- How GIS is used in emergency management.
- Tools available to enhance GIS usefulness.

This course is designed for individuals who supervise emergency management mitigation, planning, response, and recovery operations.


# Course Objectives

After completing the course you should be able to:

- Describe the types of products that GIS can produce.
- Explain the role that GIS plays in supporting emergency management through each mission area.

While the course will not promote specific GIS solutions, it will:

- Provide an overview of the types of technology options that are currently available.
- Equip you with a list of questions and issues that you should consider when choosing the best solution for your organization.


# Course Structure

The course content is divided into six lessons. To help you keep track of your place within the course, the current lesson title will be displayed in the upper left corner of each screen. In addition, a lesson list will be presented at the beginning and end of each lesson.

| Lesson | Description |
| --- | --- |
| Introduction and Course Overview | Describes procedures for completing this course and presents the course goal, objectives, and topics to be covered. |

| GIS Fundamentals | Introduces basic information about GIS capabilities. |
| GIS for Emergency Management | Introduces ways that GIS can be used as an aid to emergency management. |
| GIS Queries | Introduces the types of queries that are available using GIS and strategies for developing queries. |
| Specialized GIS Tools and Off-the-Shelf Products | Introduces specialized GIS tools and "off-the-shelf" products that can help you complete specific analyses. |
| Course Summary | Summarizes the key points in this course to prepare you for the final exam. |

## Lesson Overview and Objectives

This lesson introduces GIS, describes several uses for GIS in emergency management, and identifies some tools that can enhance the usefulness of GIS information.

At the end of this lesson, you should be able to:

- Define basic GIS terms and concepts.
- Describe how GIS is used in emergency management.
- Identify two tools that can be used to enhance GIS information.

## How Did GIS Get Its Start?

Use of GIS dates back 150 years! In 1854, Dr. John Snow analyzed geographic data to identify the source of a city-wide cholera epidemic in London.

He obtained the most accurate city map available, then plotted the known information about the outbreak. Dr. Snow knew the addresses of the people who had gotten sick and the dates their symptoms began. He also plotted the locations of known wells. By analyzing the information on his map, he was able to identify a contaminated well as the origin of the outbreak.

# What Is GIS Today?

Modern-day GIS is:

- The hardware, software, and methods that allow people to capture, store, manipulate, analyze, manage, and present geographically referenced data.
- A spatial data-management tool made up of "intelligent" computer maps linked to databases that describe map features.

GIS can be used to generate a wide array of data in a variety of applications.

# GIS: More Than a Map

Most people think of GIS in terms of maps because maps are the most familiar way to visualize spatial relationships. GIS is much more than maps, though. GIS relates different types of information in terms of their spatial relationships and reaches conclusions about those relationships.

GIS allows you to create, manipulate, and analyze data in a wide variety of ways. Imagine being able to do all the things that you can do to organize and categorize data in a spreadsheet or database, but also assign coordinates (specific points in space) to each bit of data. After the data are organized, new relationships among the data can be reviewed on a map.

GIS functions include the ability to:

- Create and/or input data.
- Modify data.
- Store data.
- Analyze data.
- Output information.
- Distribute data and information.

Each of these functions will be covered in more detail later in this course.

# Other Emergency Management Uses of GIS

GIS also can support detailed operations-level planning, implementation, training, and resources-related tasks necessary to prepare for, respond to, recover from, and mitigate any disaster. Some GIS applications include:

- Developing and maintaining lists of GIS emergency support manpower with personnel location information, contact information, and specialized skills.
- Developing lists of detailed GIS data and resource requirements to support emergency management needs.
- Developing secure, redundant GIS layers of local city/county critical infrastructure data, including a DVD set of critical data with integrated data viewing and printing applications.

## Available GIS Tools

FEMA's Mapping and Analysis Center (MAC) has developed many GIS tools that can help personnel at all government levels as well as those in the private sector and nongovernmental organizations. Some of the tools include:

- Data sets that ensure the ability to provide customers with critical information.
- Maps produced from model output and damage assessment data.
- Maps and/or tables from FEMA Human Services, National Emergency Training Center (NETC), National Processing Service Center (NPSC), and Disaster Finance Center (DFC) data.

These and other tools will be covered in more detail in later lessons.

## Other GIS Resources Available to Emergency Managers

There are other GIS resources available to emergency managers that have been developed by public and private sources. Some of these resources include:

- Customized data sets of local resources.
- Maps produced to model impacts from likely event scenarios.
- Data collection tools for damage assessment data, etc.

Additional tools are under development. Emergency managers should keep abreast of new tools that may help with any phase of emergency management.

# Lesson Summary

You have completed the Introduction and Course Overview lesson. This lesson presented:

- What GIS is and how it has evolved over time.
- Some ways in which GIS is used in emergency management.
- Some of the tools that are available to enhance GIS usefulness.

# Lesson 2: GIS Fundamentals

## Lesson Overview and Objectives

This lesson introduces basic information about GIS capabilities.

At the end of this lesson, you should be able to:

- Define GIS components.
- Name and describe two GIS data types.
- Name and describe two GIS data features.
- Analyze a scenario to identify the GIS capabilities described.

## GIS Components

Remember that Dr. John Snow first used GIS to track a cholera outbreak in London. The same components that Dr. Snow used to solve his problem remain the basis of GIS today. Fortunately, computers allow a much greater application of each component.

This lesson will describe how modern GIS uses three main components:

- Base map
- Input data
- Analysis methods and tools

## GIS Base Map

GIS allows you to create an accurate map suitable for specific purposes. Throughout the world a vast amount of spatial information has been collected and stored as layers that can be superimposed on each other to create the precise view required.

GIS allows each layer to be downloaded, then manipulated until the desired map is created. These layers can be viewed in any combination and turned on or off to achieve new combinations or connections with other layers.

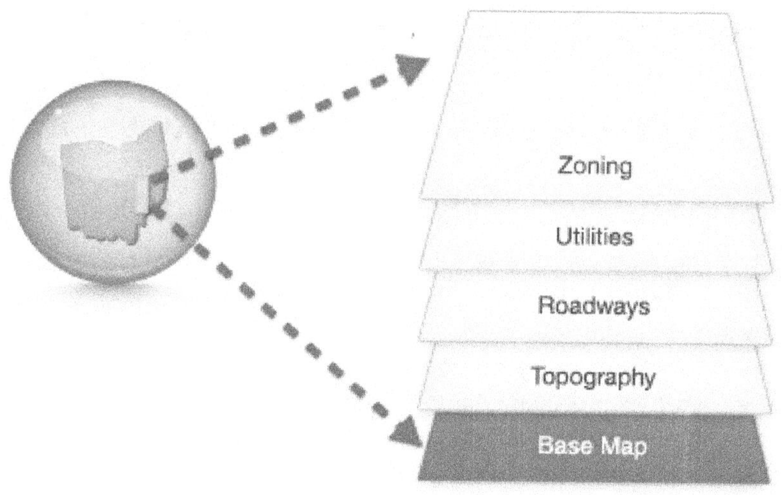


## Typical Base Map Features

A typical base map may include:

- Aerial photography.
- Streams.
- Jurisdictional boundaries.
- Streets.
- Other information, such as zoning boundaries, contours, soil types, etc.

The data for each layer are readily available in nearly all areas of the United States by contacting the local GIS vendor that produces and/or maintains them for the jurisdiction.

# Input Data

Input data can be collected on almost anything and can be linked to at least one, and usually several, geographic locations. Most input data have already been **georeferenced**—that is, the data have been linked digitally to a geographic location.

GIS data can be grouped into two categories:

- Raster data
- Vector data

There are three types of input data:

- Point data
- Aggregate data
- Line data

# GIS Data Types

GIS data can be grouped into one of two categories:

- **Raster data** are made up of thousands of individual pixels merged to create a digital image (e.g., a photograph). The smaller the pixel, the higher or more detailed the resolution of the image becomes.
- **Vector data** includes the points, lines, and polygons that represent the locations and/or boundaries of map features. Vector data would be used for:
    - Mapping streams.
    - Showing detailed twists and turns.
    - Depicting roads or utilities.
    - Identifying exact intersections.
    - Pinpointing the exact location of an elevation measurement.

# Point Data

Point data include any items that can be pinpointed on a map. Examples of point data may include:

- Locations of key infrastructure (e.g., fire halls, precinct houses, hospitals, shelters).
- Community assets (e.g., the locations of road salt or earth-moving equipment).

# Aggregate Data

Aggregate data can be aggregated by any geography (e.g., census block, city boundary). Aggregate data are typically used to protect an individual's privacy such as when:

- Mapping repetitive-loss facilities.
- There is not enough information available to represent the data with pinpoint accuracy (such as when mapping patients during an outbreak where patient addresses cannot be used so information analysis, such as by zip code, would be necessary).

The U.S. Census Bureau often releases demographic data in an aggregated form.

# Line Data

Line data may include the edges of features such as roadways or linear elements such as pipelines. They also may be used to represent aerial data features. For example many communities create a road centerline to represent the roads seen on aerial photography. Each road feature would include the name of the road and other important information.

Another example of line data is using jurisdictional boundaries as a reference. City limits, State boundaries, and county/parrish/tribal boundaries are represented by line data.

Each point, line, and area that is used as input data contains information about the feature aside from just its location. These data are dynamically generated and automatically update each time the GIS database is updated with new information.

# GIS Characteristics

GIS exhibits three main characteristics:

- Map projection
- Accuracy
- Digital orthophotography resolution

# GIS Characteristics: Map Projection

When representing the surface of a sphere or other three-dimensional shape on a two-dimensional surface, distortion necessarily occurs. To correct for the distortion and create an accurate map, the **map projection** used to develop each layer must be known.

Regardless of the map projection, all points on each map layer are correlated to those on other layers and can be corrected to correct the distortion.

As shown below, there are four ways that map projection can be distorted.

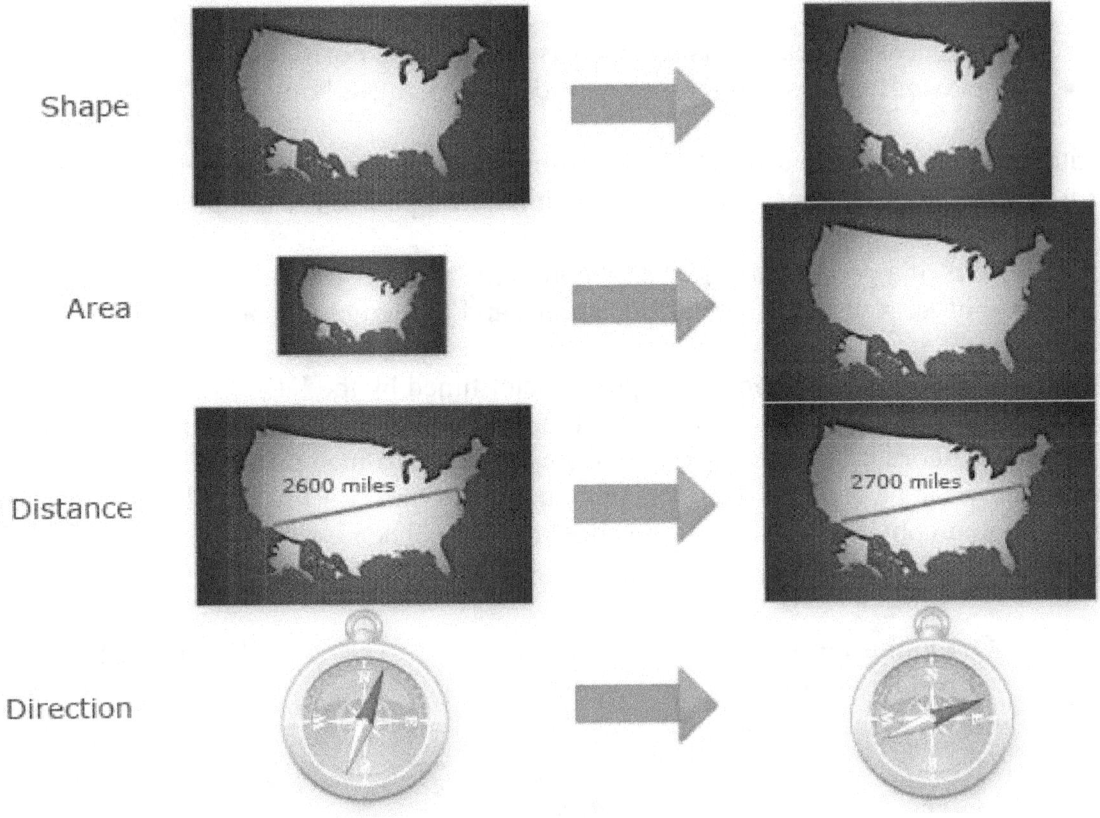


# GIS Characteristics: Accuracy

A **Digital Elevation Model (DEM)** is the representation of the earth's surface and includes elevation as well as latitude and longitude points (X, Y, Z coordinates). As more points are added to the model, the DEM becomes more accurate. The DEM is used to adjust aerial photography to real-world coordinates.

Removing distortions from camera angle and topography equalizes the distances represented on the image.

These scale-rectified aerial photographs are called **orthophotos.**

# GIS Characteristics: Digital Orthophotography

Digital orthophotos, also known as aerial photographs, combine the image characteristics of a photograph with the geometric qualities of a map. Unlike a standard aerial photograph, relief displacement in orthophotos has been removed so that ground features are displayed in their true ground position. This display allows for:

- Direct measurement of distance, areas, angles, and positions.
- Display of features that may be omitted or generalized on maps.

Digital orthophotos serve a variety of purposes, from interim maps to field references for earth science investigations and analyses. Digital orthophotos are useful as:

- Layers of a geographic information system.
- A tool for revision of digital line graphs and topographic maps.

The accuracy of digital orthophotography is determined by the DEM. Its resolution is determined by the combination of camera type and altitude at which the photography was captured. Most orthophotography varies from 1 meter to 6 inch pixels. The 1-meter pixel photography can be used for many planning activities that don't require great detail. The 6-inch photography is used for very detailed mapping. The resolution for 6-inch photography is so high that you can typically see manhole covers.

| **Orthophotography Pixel Resolution** | **Zoom In** | **Zoom In Closer** |
|---|---|---|
| | | Highly pixelated |

**1 meter**

- Good/medium resolution.
- Uses include emergency management, planning, data verification and updates, large-scale analysis,

change
direction.
- Smaller file
  sizes.

**1 foot**

- High resolution.
- Uses include
  emergency
  management,
  parcel and utility
  mapping, data
  verification and
  updates.
- Larger file sizes.

**6 inch**

- Very high
  resolution.
- Uses include
  detailed project-
  level
  infrastructure
  mapping.
- Largest file
  sizes.

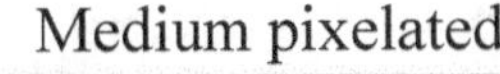
Medium pixelated

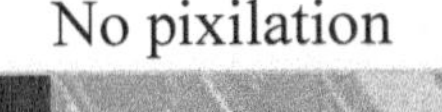
No pixilation

# Using Digital Orthophotography

Digital orthophotography is used to identify specific features (e.g., roads or the outlines of buildings) and to trace them to create other highly accurate individual layers.

The process of creating new layers by tracing on top of the photography is called **planimetrics.** The image at the right shows how the building outlines have been drawn from the orthophotography.

By creating planimetrics from current orthophotography, analysis and modeling can be done with the data. Without the processing planimetrics, they are only photos.

# GIS Database

The GIS database is a map with a unique number, or identifier. Target data can be located using database queries, such as "greater than," "less than," "sounds like," "before," etc.

Multiple databases containing a variety of attributes can be joined together and linked to geographic locations as long as there is a unique identifier for each entry that is common to both datasets.

For example, the GIS parcel database can only provide a Property Identification number. Merging with the second database through the common PropertyID address field yields the address, year built, and value of the land and building improvements. This technique allows linkage among increasing amounts of information to locations on the map.

## CAMA

| Property ID | 291402014025000006 |
|---|---|
| Property Address | 7355 Catboat Ct |
| City | Fishers |
| State | IN |
| Zip | 46038 |
| Year Built | 2010 |
| Assessed Value Land | 47000 |
| Assessed Value Improvements | 222700 |

# Lesson Summary

You have completed the GIS Fundamentals lesson. This lesson described how to:

- Define GIS components.
- Name and describe two GIS data types.
- Name and describe two GIS data features.
- Analyze a scenario to identify the GIS capabilities described.

# Lesson 3: GIS for Emergency Management

## Lesson Overview and Objectives

This lesson will introduce ways in which GIS can be used as an aid to emergency management.

At the end of this lesson, you should be able to:

- Describe how GIS is used in emergency management.
- Review scenarios to determine how GIS might be used to solve emergency management issues.

## Uses of GIS in Emergency Management

Since its development as an automated system, GIS has served emergency management well. GIS can provide the information needed to support decisionmaking before a disaster. During the early response period, emergency managers use GIS as a key intelligence source for the information they need to make decisions. And as the response moves toward recovery, GIS can identify those in greatest need to manage priorities.

## GIS Map Data

GIS maps can provide a wide array of data for emergency managers, including:

- Storm track and damage prediction.
- Wind damage prediction.
- Earthquake damage prediction.
- Counties that have been declared major disasters.
- Demographic information for an identified area.
- Road, rail, and utility locations.
- Essential facility, shelters, and other critical locations.
- Repetitive losses.
- Superfund locations.
- Shelter locations.
- Critical facility locations.

# How Is GIS Used Within FEMA?

GIS is widely used for emergency management purposes. FEMA's Mapping and Analysis Center (MAC) uses GIS to disseminate geographic information to Emergency Support Function (ESF) 5, Information and Planning, during disaster operations. FEMA is expanding its use of GIS to provide a full range of GIS services to all FEMA program offices.

# Using GIS for Emergency Management

GIS is used to support emergency management—**not** to change or replace a jurisdiction's existing Emergency Operations Plan (EOP). While the EOP addresses hazards most likely to affect an area, GIS is a supporting technology to all EOP elements.

Using GIS to support emergency management may require the use of unfamiliar analysis methods. The benefits of these new analyses will be illustrated through brief case studies on the follow screens. To be successful, GIS applications do not need to be highly technical or complex. In fact, simple is better. Whenever there is a need for a diagram or map to improve communication during an incident or emergency, think GIS.

# Using GIS for Mitigation

Mitigation activities seek to:

- Reduce the effects of a future disaster.
- Lessen the likelihood of experiencing damaging effects from an incident.
- Eliminate the possibility of being affected.

GIS provides an easy-to-use tool to help identify both the hazards and the critical infrastructure. Then through analysis, GIS helps with assessment and mitigation of the risks these hazards pose to residents and infrastructure.

The Federal Disaster Mitigation Act of 2000 (DMA2K) mandated local governments to develop and adopt a Multi-Hazard Mitigation Plan (MHMP). The MHMP should include a risk assessment and mitigation strategies to maintain eligibility for certain Federal disaster assistance and hazard mitigation funding programs. Communities participating in the National Flood Insurance Program (NFIP) must adopt the MHMP to receive mitigation funds.

The DMA2K risk assessment requires GIS data and analyses to identify the community's critical facilities and estimate potential risk. The best information to estimate risk is information contained in the city and county GIS, which includes roads, municipal boundaries, parcels, and addresses. This information can be linked to assessors' data to provide building value, square footage, and building use (residential, commercial, etc.) to calculate which assets are at greatest risk.

Also, GIS is required to locate and analyze the community's essential facilities including schools, police, fire departments, care facilities, and emergency operations centers.

# Example: Emergency Action Plan (EAP) for a High Hazard Dam

Hazards posed from dams are classified according to the potential risk to human life and potential risk of economic and/or environmental losses.

- **Low hazard (L)** means that failure or incorrect operation of the dam will result in no loss of human life and very minimal economic or environmental losses; losses are primarily limited to the owner's property.
- **Significant hazard (S)** means that failure or incorrect operation results in no probable loss of human life. It can cause economic loss, environment damage, and disruption of lifeline facilities. Dams classified as significant hazard potential dams are often located in predominantly rural or agricultural areas, but could be located in populated areas with a significant amount of infrastructure.
- **High hazard (H)** means that failure or incorrect operation has a very high risk and can result in loss of human life and significant damage to buildings and infrastructure.

The EAP defines a protocol to respond to different levels of risk for dam failure and seeks to mitigate loss of property and lives. The EAP includes GIS analyses and data that define the dam breach extent. Orthophotography, local parcel, and E911 address data can be used with the inundation maps to help emergency managers plan evacuation routes for at-risk residents.

# GIS Uses for Planning, Training, and Exercising

Planning encompasses those actions by which team members conduct a risk analysis, develop the EOP, and take actions to develop and maintain a state of readiness. GIS can support detailed operations-level planning, training, and exercising by:

- Developing and conducting training and exercise programs for GIS Unit staff.
- Developing lists of detailed GIS data and resource requirements to support emergency management needs.

- Developing secure and redundant GIS layers of local, city, or county critical infrastructure data, including a DVD set of critical data with integrated data viewing and printing application.

# Example: Introducing First Responders to GIS

An excellent first step to introduce your first responders to GIS is to geospatially enable the creation and maintenance of your existing map books (e.g., fire maps) to support daily emergency management operations. GIS map books can be printed and handed out to first responders and volunteers or exported as PDF files for Web download, viewing, and printing on demand.

Keeping map books up to date and accurate is a continual challenge. However, by using GIS software to leverage the existing GIS base map data layers that are readily available and being maintained by Federal, State, or local government sources, map books can be produced to maintain first responder map books more efficiently than ever.

Following provision of fire maps to first responders, tabletop exercises provide GIS practitioners with hands-on experience using GIS activities in an emergency situation.

Many jurisdictions across the country hold tabletop exercises for first responders and GIS personnel. Through the tabletop exercises, emergency managers and others are realizing that GIS technology and data are critical to emergency management.

# Using GIS for Response

Of all the preparedness processes, GIS is especially valuable during response. During response GIS helps emergency managers and responders by:

- Mapping incident location to help assess the incident scope, magnitude, and extent of damage.
- Coordinating resource management.
- Mapping critical infrastructure to support response efforts.
- Fulfilling real-time incident map requests to support response information needs.

# Case Study: Using GIS for Response

On September 20, 2002, a severe storm with numerous tornadoes ripped through central Indiana, resulting in damage to more than 1,200 structures across the State, including Marion County (Indianapolis).

The Indianapolis Mapping and Geographic Infrastructure System (IndyGIS), in collaboration with the Department of Metropolitan Development, Indianapolis EMA, and the Department of Public Works, mapped the locations of damaged and destroyed structures by:

- Establishing a centralized system to coordinate data collection and distribution.
- Providing real-time data to all players to support the response effort.
- Using digital ortho/oblique aerial photography quickly after the event.

By collecting and mapping the locations of damaged structures, IndyGIS was able to generate initial damage estimates. The State used this information to expedite the Federal request for an emergency declaration.

The initial data collected to identify and quantify the location of damaged and destroyed structures came through the traditional public safety response channels (e.g., phone calls, notes created based on onsite visits). The team entered the handwritten notes into a spreadsheet, then migrated data from the spreadsheet to a database. Finally, data from the database were geocoded onto the IndyGIS database.

The response mapping process started by establishing a map grid to cover the area, and creating printed 8.5" x 11" damage assessment maps for the Emergency Operations Center and field crews to use.

In addition to mapping the location of damaged and destroyed structures, the Indianapolis EMA used GIS for evacuation routing analysis, and for identifying businesses that housed volatile chemicals.

# Using GIS in Recovery

Recovery includes all tasks necessary to return to predisaster function. GIS uses during recovery include developing maps to:

- Implement demobilization procedures, coordinate recovery, and restore unused resources.
- Provide required documentation for cost recovery to the Federal and State governments.
- Support after-action reporting and subsequent planning efforts.

# Case Study: Using GIS for Recovery

As part of the city of New Orleans recovery efforts after Hurricane Katrina, the city's Office of Technology developed the One New Orleans Community Recovery & Resources Web Page to present easy-to-find, concise, comprehensive data online about the recovery and rebuilding of New Orleans.

By leveraging the city of New Orleans' existing GIS data coupled with new field inventory data and imagery collected during the Katrina response and recovery efforts, a number of interactive Web maps were made available to the community so people could see the status or report on their individual homesteads. These interactive maps were directly tied to other online applications so that the reporting and recovery efforts link directly to existing city services.

After this initial deployment, the One New Orleans Community Recovery & Resources initiative has now made emergency preparedness a permanent feature that is front and center on the city's Web site.

The new site is an integrated part of the city's day-to-day business and provides community resources to support the entire disaster life cycle. Several applications on this site are linked directly into leveraging the city's existing GIS data.


# Other Emergency Management Uses of GIS

GIS also can support detailed operations-level planning, implementation, training, and resources-related tasks necessary to prepare for, respond to, recover from, and mitigate any disaster. Some GIS action items include:

- Developing and maintaining lists of GIS emergency support manpower with personnel location information, contact information, and specialized skills.
- Developing lists of detailed GIS data and resource requirements to support emergency management needs.
- Developing secure, redundant GIS layers of local city/county critical infrastructure data, including a DVD set of critical data with integrated data viewing and printing applications.

# Available GIS Tools

FEMA's Mapping and Analysis Center (MAC) has developed many GIS tools that can help personnel at all government levels as well as those in the private sector and nongovernmental organizations. Some of the tools include:

- Data sets that ensure the ability to provide customers with critical information.
- Maps produced from model output, damage assessment data.
- Maps and/or tables from FEMA Human Services, National Emergency Training Center (NETC), National Processing Services Center (NPSC), and Disaster Finance Center (DFC) data.

These and other tools will be covered in more detail in later lessons.


# Lesson Summary

You have completed the GIS for Emergency Management lesson. This lesson described:

- The types of information GIS can provide.
- How GIS can be used in various scenarios during all mission areas.

# Lesson 4: GIS Queries

## Lesson Overview and Objectives

This lesson introduces the types of queries that are available using GIS and describes strategies for developing queries.

At the end of this lesson, you should be able to:

- Select the best type of query available to produce specific types of information.
- Describe strategies for querying GIS efficiently.
- Explain how data sets are used for querying GIS.

## GIS Queries

After data have been placed on a map, GIS allows users to sort and filter them in a way that can answer questions about how the data relate to other data.

For example, to find schools located in a floodplain, GIS can be queried and report only those schools that are at risk.

GIS can answer these and other questions through its query function, which is described in this lesson.

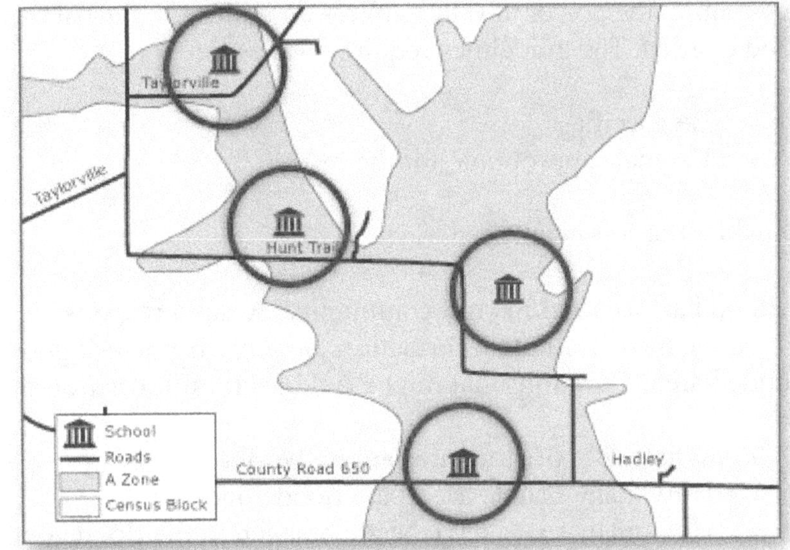

# GIS Queries

GIS queries can help you answer many different questions. These questions include:

- Where is something located?
- What locations meet certain criteria?
- What locations are within a specific region or area?
- What is the safety zone around a location?
- Is there a relationship between or among GIS layers?
- Has a region changed over time?

This lesson will enable you to develop queries that will provide the information you need from GIS.

# Creating Good Queries

Leveraging the power of GIS requires an understanding of the guidelines for forming good queries. The guidelines require queries to:

- Be specific.
- Use data appropriate for the query.

Consider the following scenario:

A flood has occurred in your community. A rapid response is required. GIS can help you obtain the most accurate information, but only if you ask good questions about the flooded area. Questions that might yield useful information in this situation include:

- What types of structures are in the flood zone?
- How many people are in the flood zone?
- How many roads have been damaged in the flood zone?

Why? The questions developed in this scenario will yield accurate information because:

- Knowing the types of structures that are in the flood zone can help generate more questions about specific structures in the flood zone.
- Knowing how many people are in the flood zone can help address the needs of the entire population affected, and also identify whether any people with access and functional needs, such as those living in nursing homes, are at risk.
- Knowing the number of damaged roads in the flood zone can help identify whether access routes have been blocked by flooding.

# Introduction to GIS Data Sets

Examples of data sets that have been developed to make GIS queries easier include the following:

**Transportation**

**Purpose:** Identify access routes to an incident, evacuation routes, and other related transportation reference points. Support routing of public vehicles (evacuation/avoidance).

- Streets, which are sometimes referred to as a "Centerline File" (name, hierarchy: primary vs. interstate)
- Private roads
- Traffic control points
- Access control points
- Road construction
- Transportation resources: buses, school buses (with wheelchair access), ambulances
- Navigable waterways
- Mass transit
- Railways
- Airports
- Helicopter landing zones

**Population**

**Purpose:** Identify impacted and at-risk populations.

- Daytime population
- At-risk populations (schools, daycare centers, public meeting places, senior citizen homes, universities, etc.)

**Buildings**

**Purpose:** Identify affected facilities in use for the incident.

- Potential shelter sites (large buildings, schools, convention centers, etc.)
- Primary and secondary mass care centers from existing emergency operations center plans
- Critical infrastructure
- Building footprints
- Ice arenas (temporary morgues)

**Utilities**

**Purpose:** Identify infrastructure that could be damaged or hazardous. Provide guidance for access by first responders.

- Utility pipelines
- Power lines (underground and overhead)
- Propane farms
- Sanitary sewers
- Water treatment plants
- Storm water facilities: catch basins, storm sewers outfalls
- Fire hydrants
- Potable water mains
- Public service facilities (public works, water treatment, waste water treatment, electrical plants)

**Communications**

**Purpose:** Identify potential communication outages due to the incident.

- Cell towers
- Radio communication
- Siren locations, sound buffers
- Main Internet hubs/lines

**Land Ownership/Administrative**

**Purpose:** Identify land ownership. These data may be managed by the tax assessor's office.

- Address points
- Parcel boundaries
- Jurisdictions

## Environment

**Purpose:** Identify physical environment conditions that may influence hazard behavior or response.

- Topography
- Water courses
- Lakes
- Rivers
- Department of environmental management
- Fuel models
- Historical fire incidents
- FEMA flood zones
- Extremely Hazardous Sites and Hazardous Sites (SARA Title 3 sites)

## Imagery

**Purpose:** View predisaster images of current features.

- Aerial imagery with date
- Oblique aerial imagery (e.g., pictometry)

## Dynamic Datasets

**Purpose:** Gain perspective on incident within context of current conditions.

- Atmospheric conditions (wind direction, etc.)
- Traffic counts/traffic flow
- Incident data sets

## Incident Specific

**Purpose:** Visualize location and extent of incident.

- Location and extent of tactical area or incident boundaries (point, line, or polygon)
- Plume (fire, chemical, etc.)
- Earthquake maps (USGS)

**Incident Command**

**Purpose:** Identify incident operations sites and zones.

- Incident command post
- Staging areas
- Hot/warm/cold zones
- Shelter sites
- Decontamination site
- Evacuation zone
- Police/fire stations
- Hospitals/emergency care
- Heliports
- Airports
- Landmarks

Source: GIS Standard Operating Guidance for Multi-Agency Coordination Centers
Version 1.0 January 2011

# Analyzing GIS Data

Even with appropriate queries and good output data, the usefulness of the data will be minimized without analyzing the data.

# Simple GIS Analysis

For queries that will be repeated frequently but with different parameters within various geographic areas, simple interfaces can be created. These interfaces allow the end user to search complex datasets and produce significant results. The map below illustrates the results of a simple GIS interface.

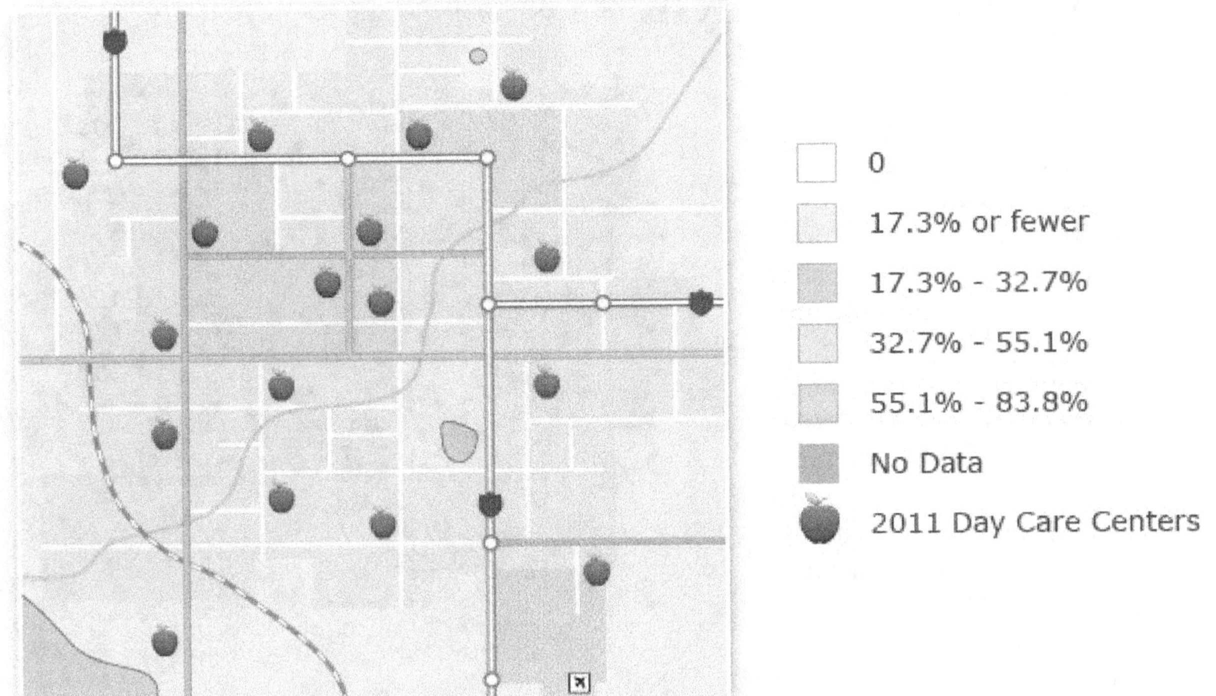

Note: Used with permission from SAVI.



GIS also can analyze many different data layers together based on specific criteria, such as:

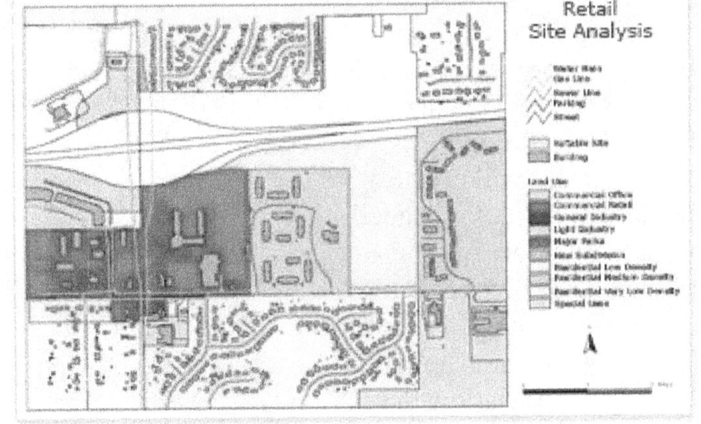



- Proximity to utility lines.
- Residential neighborhoods.
- Roads.
- Adherence to land use (e.g., to find suitable sites for retail development).

# Repeatable GIS Analysis

For queries that will be repeated frequently with different parameters and within various geographic areas, simple interfaces can be created. These interfaces allow the end user to search complex datasets and produce significant results. Some communities have Web sites to generate these simple queries and overlays.

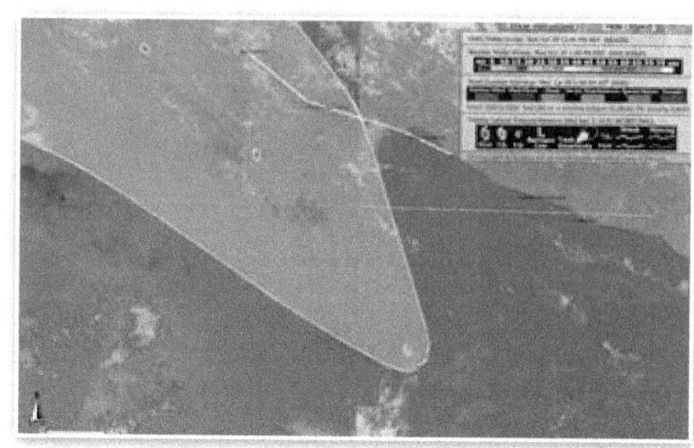

The map shown here is a screen from the Hurricane Evacuation (HURREVAC) model, which is used to help determine whether an evacuation should be ordered. For example, an application may be customized to query daycare providers and young single mothers within a specific geographic area. Assuming the user chooses to display the number of single mothers under 25 years old by census tract, the analysis automatically will create a thematic map (color shaded based on number of single mothers under 25 years old). The user then chooses daycare centers, which are shown on the map. The relationships between daycare locations to locations of young single mothers can be analyzed quickly.

Using a custom community information system, data are dynamically generated in community profiles and automatically updated each

time the database receives new
information.

Map used with permission
from SAVI.

# Using GIS Data

The following example of GIS
analysis would potentially be very
valuable for emergency managers. In
this analysis, the GIS analyst
determined which mobile home
parks within the city of Indianapolis
should receive emergency shelters.

The analyst created a feature layer
containing mobile home parks
throughout the city, adding attributes
denoting the physical condition of
infrastructure. These data, combined
with a feature layer showing
historical tornado paths, allowed the
analyst to run a simple analysis that
identified which areas were at the
most risk of suffering severe damage
from a future tornado event.

Mobile home parks determined to
have the highest risk were prioritized
to receive emergency shelters.

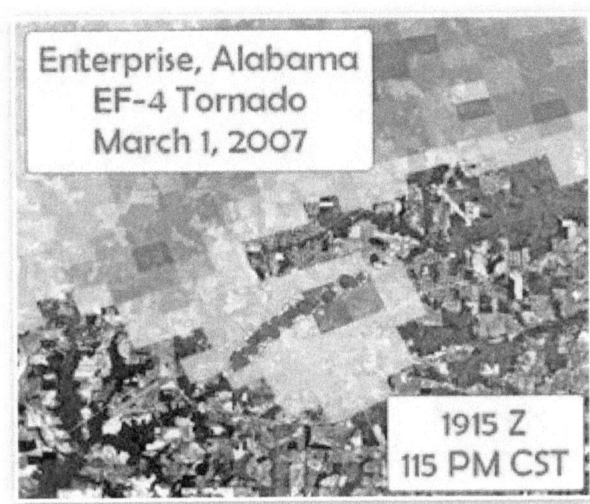


Example of a query result

# Lesson Summary

You have completed the GIS Queries lesson. This lesson described:

- How to develop good questions for querying GIS.
- Datasets that can be used when querying GIS.
- Different types of queries.
- Ways to analyze queries.

# Lesson 5: Specialized GIS Tools and Off-the-Shelf Products

## Lesson Overview and Objectives

This lesson introduces specialized GIS tools and off-the-shelf products that can help you complete specific analyses.

After completing this lesson, you should be able to:

- Identify a variety of tools and resources to support your GIS needs.
- List specific scenarios to which you may apply these tools and resources.

## GIS Resources

There is a variety of Federal, State, and local resources to support GIS needs. Those resources include:

- Hazus Multi-Hazards (MH).
- Areal Locations of Hazardous Atmospheres (ALOHA).
- Spread projections.
- Geo-Targeted Alerting System (GTAS).

## GIS Resources: Hazus-MH

Hazus-MH is FEMA's powerful risk assessment software program. Hazus-MH is used for analyzing potential losses from floods, hurricane winds, and earthquakes. It combines current scientific and engineering knowledge with the latest GIS technology to produce estimates of hazard-related damage before or after a disaster occurs.

**Hazus-MH Fact Sheet**

| Hazus-MH | |
|---|---|
| **Description** | The Hazards U.S. Multi-Hazard (Hazus-MH) is a GIS software package that uses census data and other existing databases to estimate damage and losses from earthquakes, hurricane winds, and floods. |

| | |
|---|---|
| | Hazus-MH contains an extensive inventory of data for every community in the United States that can help users conduct loss estimation in a timely, cost-efficient manner. Hazus-MH also allows users to update and add location-specific data, as well as overlay information about other hazards on the maps. |
| **Use** | Hazus-MH has evolved into a powerful tool for mitigation and recovery planning and analysis. An increasing number of States, localities, and tribes are using Hazus-MH in the preparation of risk assessments and mitigation plans under the Disaster Mitigation Act of 2000. Hazus-MH is also being used to support postdisaster planning for recovery from hurricanes, earthquakes, and floods.<br><br>Hazus-MH can be used by individuals and organizations with limited knowledge of hazard analysis, as well as by those with extensive expertise in the earth, building, and GIS sciences due to its diverse range of options.<br><br>Hazus-MH is used for mitigation and recovery as well as preparedness and response. Government planners, GIS specialists, and emergency managers use Hazus-MH to determine losses and the most beneficial mitigation approaches to take to minimize them. Hazus-MH can be used in the assessment step in the mitigation planning process, which is the foundation for a community's long-term strategy to reduce disaster losses and break the cycle of disaster damage, reconstruction, and repeated damage. Being ready will aid in recovery after a natural disaster. |
| **Obtaining Hazus** | Federal, State, local, and tribal agencies and the private sector can order the latest version of Hazus free of charge online by visiting the FEMA Map Service Center (MSC) Web Store at http://www.msc.fema.gov. |

Hazus-MH analyzes input data to estimate losses. The graphic shown here illustrates the Hazus analysis workflow (from bottom to top) to assess potential risk from hazards.

# Hazus-MH Step 1: Analyze Physical Landscape

Step 1, hazard analysis, begins with an assessment of the environment and includes factors such as soil composition for earthquakes, terrain changes for flooding, and land cover for hurricanes.

# Hazus-MH Step 2: Identify Hazards

During Step 2, Hazus-MH assesses specified hazards. For example, Hazus may identify a 5.5 magnitude earthquake, or a flood event caused by a 10-inch rain over 8 hours, as being among high-risk hazards for the defined area.

# Hazus-MH Step 3: Consider What Is at Risk

After identifying hazards for which a jurisdiction is at risk, Hazus completes an additional analysis to determine what is at risk in the community. For example:

- Which buildings would be damaged or destroyed?
- Which population(s) would be at risk?

# Hazus-MH Step 4: Analyze Social and Economic Impacts

Next, Hazus calculates the estimated losses that would result if the structures and populations identified in Step 3 were damaged.

# Hazus-MH Step 5: Produce Maps, Tables, and Reports

The final step reflects the output of the model, which includes maps, tables, and reports to summarize the analysis results.

# Hazus-MH Data

The Hazus software includes data for **every** census block in the United States.

- Demographic data from the U.S. Census Bureau provide estimates of income, population, demographics, occupancies, and housing unit development.
- U.S. Census Bureau and Dun & Bradstreet data provide information about the general building stock inventory.
- Department of Energy (DOE) data define regional variations in characteristics such as number and size of garages, types of building foundations, and number of stories within a building.

In addition to aggregate data, Hazus contains site-specific data for essential and high-profile facilities.

The more site-specific data you incorporate into Hazus, the more accurate your analysis results will be. However, more specific data analysis will also require additional training and GIS resources.

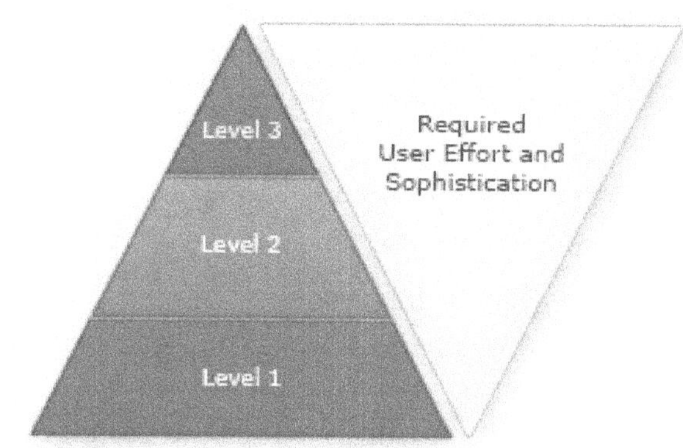


# GIS Resources: ALOHA

Plume/elliptical modeling programs, such as the National Oceanic and Atmospheric Administration's (NOAA's) Areal Locations of Hazardous Atmospheres (ALOHA), are predictors of airborne plumes for incident scenarios, including fires, HAZMAT, and biological/chemical/radiological release.

**ALOHA Fact Sheet**

## ALOHA

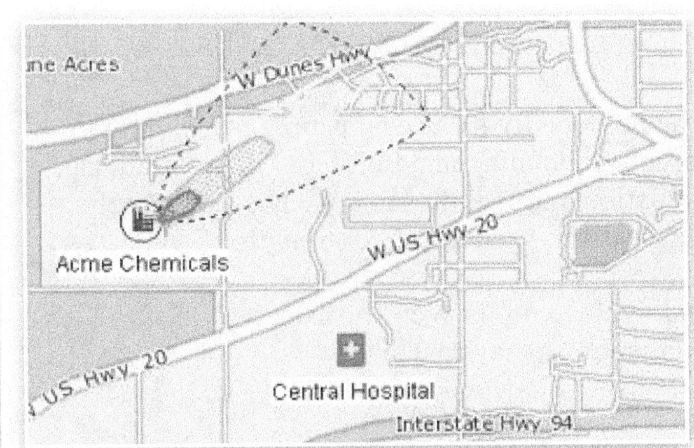


ALOHA (Areal Locations of Hazardous Atmospheres) is a modeling program that estimates threat zones associated with hazardous chemical releases, including toxic gas clouds, fires, and explosions. A threat zone is an area where a hazard (such as toxicity, flammability, thermal radiation, or damaging overpressure) has exceeded a user-specified Level of Concern (LOC).

An ALOHA threat zone plot displayed on a MARPLOT map. The red, orange, and yellow zones indicate areas where specific Level of Concern thresholds were exceeded.

ALOHA was developed jointly by NOAA and the Environmental Protection Agency (EPA), and it runs on both Macintosh and Windows computers.

**Key Program Features**

- Generates a variety of scenario-specific output, including threat zone plots, threat at specific locations, and source strength graphs.
- Calculates the rate of release for chemicals escaping from tanks, puddles (on both land and water), and gas pipelines and predicts how that release rate changes over time.
- Models many release scenarios: toxic gas clouds, BLEVEs (Boiling Liquid Expanding Vapor Explosions), jet fires, vapor cloud explosions, and pool fires.
- Evaluates different types of hazard (depending on the release scenario): toxicity, flammability, thermal radiation, and overpressure.
- Displays threat zones on Mapping Applications for Response, Planning, and Local Operational Tasks (MARPLOT) maps (and on ArcView and ArcMap with the Arc Tool extensions).

- Works seamlessly with companion programs Computer-Aided Management of Emergency Operations (CAMEO) Chemicals and MARPLOT; it can also be used as a standalone program.

ALOHA can be obtained at: http://www.epa.gov/osweroe1/content/cameo/aloha.htm

ALOHA is a computer program designed especially for use by people responding to chemical accidents, as well as for emergency planning and training. The program can be used with GIS to help quantify the population and facilities at risk. The user simply inputs information about the chemical, atmosphere, and source strength.

ALOHA software is available for free download on its Web site as part of the CAMEO (Computer-Aided Management of Emergency Operations) suite.

# GIS Resources: Spread Projections

Spread projections are predictions for the spread of communicable diseases, infestations, fire, or other hazards over time and distance following an incident. Wildfire spread projections relate the rate of spread to weather conditions.

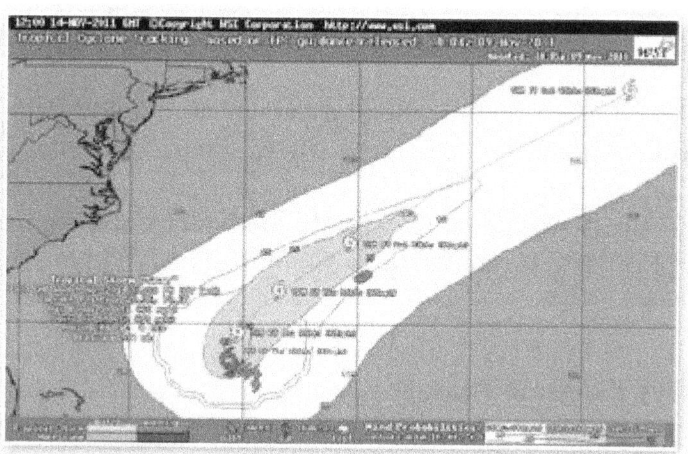

An example of a spread projection is CommunityFlu, a software program developed by the Centers for Disease Control and Prevention (CDC) that simulates the spread of influenza through a model community, and the impact of a variety of potential interventions (e.g., vaccinations, school closings, wearing of face masks, patient and household isolation/self-quarantine).

No Intervention

| Age Groups (years) | Total # Ill in Population | Number in Hospitals | Number of Deaths | Days Lost Due to Illness |
|---|---|---|---|---|
| 6-18 | 61,484 | 554 | 5 | 149,074 |
| 19-64 | 85,268 | 967 | 132 | 155,329 |
| 65+ | 12,019 | 1,968 | 1,968 | 38,148 |

|  | Totals: | 158,771 | 5,881 | 2,105 | 342,551 |

**Days Lost per Person: 0.82**

**Intervention(s)**

| Age Groups (years) | Total # Ill in Population | Number in Hospitals | Number of Deaths | Days Lost Due to Illness |
|---|---|---|---|---|
| 6-18 | 20,430 | 185 | 2 | 49,434 |
| 19-64 | 50,192 | 569 | 78 | 91,432 |
| 65+ | 66,481 | 2,351 | 1,061 | 20,570 |
| **Totals:** | **77,183** | **3,104** | **1,141** | **163,064** |

**Days Lost per Person: 0.78**

# GIS Resources: GTAS

NOAA is developing the Geo-Targeted Alerting System (GTAS) in partnership with Integrated Public Alert and Warning System (IPAWS) for plume modeling and collaboration. GTAS will quickly estimate the affected area during a HAZMAT incident using current weather conditions and allow for the rapid creation of a public alerting message. GTAS also provides collaboration tools for emergency managers to leverage the expertise of their supporting NWS Weather Forecast Office.

**GTAS Fact Sheet**

| GTAS |
|---|
| NOAA is developing the Geo-Targeted Alerting System (GTAS) in partnership with Integrated Public Alert and Warning System (IPAWS) for plume modeling and collaboration.<br><br>GTAS will quickly estimate the affected area during a HAZMAT incident using current weather conditions and allow for the rapid creation of a public alerting message. It will also provide collaboration tools for emergency managers to leverage the expertise of their supporting National Weather Service (NWS) Weather Forecast Office (WFO).<br><br>GTAS will enable emergency managers from their desktops to:<br><br><ul><li>Run and view dispersion of toxic plume information.</li><li>View hazardous weather information.</li><li>Coordinate and collaborate with NWS WFO meteorologists.</li><li>Assess societal impacts due to toxic chemical releases and severe weather conditions.</li><li>Disseminate societal impact information.</li></ul> |

- Coordinate and collaborate with other State and local emergency operations centers (EOCs).

GTAS will build upon established relationships between local NWS WFOs and local EOCs by providing shared situational awareness of vital data, so that emergency managers can quickly determine the impact and provide mitigation and response plans to the public and other local and State EOCs.

# GIS-Based Products: FEMA Flood-Related Products

The National Flood Insurance Program (NFIP) was initiated in 1968 to develop Flood Insurance Rate Maps (FIRMs), illustrating areas of flood risk to communities. In 2002, the data were digitized and enhanced using GIS through a program called Map Modernization, since renamed as Risk MAP. Risk MAP is a comprehensive plan to deliver quality data that increases public awareness and leads to actions that reduce flood risk.

Risk MAP products described in this lesson include GIS data sets that depict flood changes over time, depth grid analyses, and Hazus flood analyses.

# FEMA Flood-Related Products: Changes Since Last FIRM (CSLF)

Changes Since Last FIRM (CSLF) highlight the floodplain boundary changes a community experienced over a period of time. The results compare:

- The old 100-year flood (1 percent chance flood) boundary to . . .
- A new 100-year boundary and compare the same for the 500-year flood boundary.

This product is helpful for emergency managers because it illustrates areas that are now in the floodplain that previously were not in the floodplain. It also helps residents to determine whether or not they are eligible to receive discounted flood insurance.

# FEMA Flood-Related Products: Flood Depth Grid

The Flood Depth Grid depicts, by color, the depth of water for a 0.2 percent (500-year flood). GIS data increase flood risk awareness by communicating that risk varies within the mapped floodplain. The Flood Depth Grid also is valuable to emergency managers for planning evacuation and transportation routes.

## FEMA Flood-Related Products: Percent Chance Flood Grid

The Percent Chance Flood Grid shows the likelihood of flooding at least once within a 30-year period. Because it shows the likelihood that homeowners will experience a significant flood within the period of their 30-year mortgage, it is useful for communicating flood risk to citizens.

## GIS Data Resources

Many data resources have been developed for use with GIS. All are intended for use by trained GIS professionals to support emergency managers. Although these resources usually are implemented by others for the emergency management staff's use, it is important for key emergency management personnel to have an understanding of them to help direct the development of map products for the greater community.

## GIS Data Resources: FGDC

The Federal Geographic Data Committee (FGDC) is an organized structure of Federal geospatial professionals and constituents. FGDC provides executive, managerial, and advisory direction and oversight for geospatial decisions and initiatives across the Federal Government. The FGDC is chaired by the Secretary of the Interior with the Deputy Director for Management, OMB as Vice-Chair.

One of the major initiatives of the FGDC is the National Spatial Data Infrastructure (NSDI). The NSDI is a means to assemble geographic data nationwide to serve a variety of users. Therefore, working with any geospatial data from any Federal agency will most likely be a part of the NSDI.

## GIS Data Resources: FGDC Geospatial Platform

The partner agencies of the FGDC currently are developing a Geospatial Platform to provide place-based products and services to the American public. The Geospatial

Platform will be a managed portfolio of common geospatial data, services, and applications:

- Contributed and administered by authoritative sources.
- Hosted on a shared infrastructure.

The Geospatial Platform is used by government agencies and partners to meet their mission needs and the broader needs of the Nation.


# GIS Data Resources: USGS

The U.S. Geological Survey (USGS) is a Federal science organization that provides impartial information on the:

- Health of ecosystems and the environment.
- Natural hazard threats.
- Natural resources.
- Impacts of climate and land-use change.
- Core science systems that help provide timely, relevant, and useable information.

There are many GIS resources available through the USGS. These resources include:

- National Geospatial Program (NGP)
- National Geospatial Partnership
- The National Map
    - The National Map Viewer
    - The National Atlas of the United States
    - U.S. Topo
- Geospatial One-Stop/geodata.gov
- Geospatial Information Response Team (GIRT)
- Land Processes Distributed Active Archive Center (LP DAAC)
- USGS Seamless Data Warehouse
- USGS Emergency Operations Portal

**Job Aid: USGS and Other GIS Resources**

| **National Geospatial Program (NGP)** |
| --- |
| The NGP of the USGS manages the National Map, the National Atlas, the Geospatial One-Stop/geodata.gov, the Geospatial Information Response Team (GIRT), and other GIS resources. |

A significant objective of the NGP, through the Partnership Network, is to leverage assets through mutually beneficial partnerships that ensure the ongoing availability of current data consistent with National Spatial Data Infrastructure principles.

The National Geospatial Partnership network is comprised of the following components:

- **Partnerships and External Coordination** provides strategic direction and oversight to the range of NGP partnership activities and oversees communications, outreach, and external coordination for the program.
- **Federal Geospatial Liaisons** work with other Federal agencies to develop and manage partnerships at the national and programmatic level to support development and use of NGP products and services and the NSDI.
- **USGS Geospatial Liaisons** have been established for each State to engage and support Federal, regional, State, local, tribal, and other partners in improving timeliness, quality, and accessibility of geospatial data for the community. The USGS Geospatial Liaisons are an invaluable resource to assist State, local, and tribal governments in GIS initiatives.

## The National Map

The National Map comprises a variety of products and services that provide the Nation with access to base geospatial information to describe the landscape of the United States and its territories. The National Map (http://nationalmap.gov) supports data download, digital and print versions of topographic maps, geospatial data services, and online viewing. Customers can use geospatial data and maps to enhance their recreational experience, make life-saving decisions, support their scientific missions, and for countless other activities. Nationally consistent geospatial data from The National Map enable better policy and land management decisions and more effective enforcement of regulatory responsibilities.

Two valuable GIS resources of The National Map are the following:

- **The National Map Viewer.** More experienced map makers, as well as professional users of geographic information, should try The National Map Viewer to preview and download the data or read more about the products and services of The National Map.
- **The National Atlas of the United States.** The National Atlas of the United States enables the creation of accurate maps of America using hundreds of authoritative map themes in the National Atlas. Where The National Map is used for more detailed and technical presentations of data, the National Atlas is a "light" version that allows the creation of "high-level" thematic maps For example, in support of the same forest fire incident:
    - The National Map data could be used to map detailed firefighting information and containment plans to support the first responders.

- The National Atlas could be used to map the forest fire areas, the communities affected, and shelter locations to support public awareness.

## U.S. Topo

U.S. Topo represents the next generation of digital topographic maps from the USGS. Arranged in the traditional 7.5-minute quadrangle format, digital U.S. Topo maps are designed to look and feel like the traditional paper topographic maps for which the USGS is so well known. At the same time, U.S. Topo maps provide modern technical advantages that support wider and faster public distribution and enable basic, on-screen geographic analysis for all users.

U.S. Topo maps are available free on the Web. Each map quadrangle is constructed in GeoPDF® (i.e., products used to deliver maps and imagery from multiple U.S. Government agencies. For example, the Quadrangle map from The National Map is available from the USGS store in as GeoPDF products and is free to download. Each map quadrangle is constructed in GeoPDF® format from key layers of geographic data—orthoimagery, roads, geographic names, contours, and hydrographic features—found in The National Map, which is a nationwide collection of integrated data from local, Federal, State, and other sources.

## The Geospatial One-Stop/geodata.gov

The Geospatial One-Stop (GOS) project is an E-Government initiative, managed by the USGS. GOS promotes coordination and alignment of geospatial data collection, maintenance, and access among all levels of government. The project provides one-stop Web access to our Nation's geospatial information through development of a Data Discovery Portal (www.geodata.gov). The portal is populated by hundreds of Federal, State, local, and tribal organizations that are the creators and stewards of GIS data sets.

## The Geospatial Information Response Team (GIRT)

To assist in responding to natural and potential adversarial or human-caused disasters, the USGS has established the Geospatial Information Response Team (GIRT), which seeks to ensure rapid coordination and availability of geospatial information for effective response by emergency responders and land and resource managers. GIRT also enables better, more effective scientific analysis. GIRT is responsible for establishing and monitoring procedures for geospatial data acquisition, processing, and archiving; discovery, access, and delivery of data; anticipating geospatial needs; and providing relevant geospatial products and services.

GIRT provides important data sets for an emergency manager. For example, dynamic (live) data that can be accessed from this site include: current streamflow conditions, earthquake event shake maps, flood inundation maps, and wildfire event extent maps. Other examples of static GIS data that can be accessed include FEMA DFIRMs (Digital Flood Insurance Rate Maps), Geologic karst maps (maps showing types of rocks, sediment, etc., that are sometimes used for landslide, earthquake, and other modeling), and much more.

## The Land Processes Distributed Active Archive Center (LP DAAC)

The Land Processes Distributed Active Archive Center (LP DAAC) is a component of the National Aeronautics and Space Administration's (NASA's) Earth Observing System (EOS) and USGS Earth Resources Observation and Science (EROS) Center. NASA and USGS process, archive, and distribute land processes data received from EOS satellites, thus establishing a Distributed Active Archive Center.

This archive center provides access to data, tools, and imagery products from a number of different NASA satellite sources.

These data sets can provide valuable information when large geographic areas are affected by events such as floods (normal channels shown in gray overlaid on blue water).

## Seamless Data Warehouse

The data on The National Map Seamless Server consist of public domain orthoimagery, elevation, and land cover data. Warehouse tools provide the ability to download the GIS data layers and connect to the layers as map services.

Imagery data resolution varies by area and product. At a minimum, the Federal National Aerial Imagery Program (NAIP) provides 1-meter pixel resolution true color imagery for the continental United States. Many individual States have developed their own statewide imagery and elevation data sets at greater resolutions of half-meter or one-foot pixel resolutions. Local (county/city) government agencies may provide more current or accurate imagery data (e.g., 6-inch pixel), and should be checked first.

## Emergency Operations Portal

Explore critical predisaster and postdisaster images and data sets online for immediate viewing and downloading. The USGS Emergency Operations (http://hdds.usgs.gov/EO) in support of the Department of Homeland Security provides images for use in disaster preparations, rescue and relief operations, damage assessments, and reconstruction efforts. We supply satellite and aerial images for analysis of disaster areas before, during, and after a disaster.

The USGS Emergency Operations Portal, the LP DAAC, and the GIRT sites have similarities and overlap in the data sets that are available. The primary distinction in this portal is the availability of more event-specific imagery data products.

## The United States Department of Agriculture (USDA) & Natural Resources Conservation Services (NRCS)

The USDA maintains detailed GIS data for Agriculture and Natural Resources. The Natural Resources Conservation Services (NRCS) is the main distribution source for soils data. State Soil Geographic (STATSGO) and Soil Survey Geographic (SSURGO) soils data, as well as various status maps, are available online. STATSGO and SSURGO are the two most frequently used soils databases.

- **STATSGO** was designed primarily for regional, multistate, river basin, State, and multicounty resource planning, management, and monitoring. STATSGO:
    - Is produced by generalizing more detailed databases.
    - Is not detailed enough to make interpretations at the county level.
- **SSURGO** provides the most detailed level of information. It was designed primarily for farm and ranch, landowner, township, and/or county planning. The SSURGO database is an excellent source for determining erodible area and developing erosion control, determining land use potential, and identifying appropriate wetland areas.

## The National Oceanic and Atmospheric Administration (NOAA), Coastal Service Center (CSC)

The Coastal Service Center (CSC) works with private- and public-sector partners to address coastal issues.

In addition to the many surface GIS layers available, coastal communities have an important need for bathymetry, topography, sea surface data, and marine oceanic data to provided rescuers with valuable information. Some examples of the NOAA-provided coastal GIS data sets include:

- Charts Bathymetry and Topography.
- Electronic and Scanned Navigational Chart data.
- Marine Jurisdictions data.
- Shipping Route data.
- Forest Cover and Fragmentation data.
- Coastal IfSAR & Lidar (elevation data).
- High-Resolution Land cover data.

The CSC provides fast access to the coastal data most requested by Digital Coast partners. Access to data managed by the NOAA CSC is provided through the Data

Access Viewer, which allows for user-specified geographies, formats, and resolutions. Other data sets are provided through various mechanisms maintained by their agencies of responsibility.

## The U.S. Census Bureau

The Census Bureau serves as the leading source of quality data about the Nation's people and economy. It collects a wealth of data that are tied to geography and available for download in GIS-ready formats, including:

- Population & Housing Census: Available every 10 years
- Economic Census: Available every 5 years
- Census of Governments: Available every 5 years
- American Community Survey: Available annually
- Demographic & Economic Surveys: Ongoing

The most well-known GIS data from the Census Bureau is the TIGER/Line Shapefiles, which contain the geographic information from the Census Bureau's MAF/TIGER® (Master Address File/Topologically Integrated Geographic Encoding and Referencing) database. These data include road centerlines with address ranges, all legal boundaries and their names for statistical data collection and tabulation purposes, and census tracts and blocks. The TIGER/Line Shapefiles do not contain demographic or economic data. These data can be downloaded separately, however, using American FactFinder.

With this wealth of GIS data about our people, where they live, where they work, and their demographic and socioeconomic profiles, these data are invaluable for many applications. The Census Bureau recently released OnTheMap for Emergency Management Version 2.0. This newest version supports assessments for hurricanes, floods, and wildfires.

OnTheMap for Emergency Management is a public data tool that provides unique real-time detail on the workforce for U.S. areas affected by hurricanes, floods, and wildfires. The Web-based tool provides an intuitive interface for viewing the location and extent of current and forecasted emergency events on a map and allows users to retrieve detailed reports containing labor market characteristics for these areas. The reports provide the number and location of jobs, industry type, worker age, and earnings. Worker race, ethnicity, and educational attainment data are in beta testing at this time.

To provide users with the latest data available, OnTheMap for Emergency Management automatically incorporates real-time data updates from the National Weather Service, Departments of Interior and Agriculture, and other agencies for hurricanes, floods, and wildfires.

OnTheMap for Emergency Management Version 2.0 can be accessed by selecting "Local Employment Dynamics" at http://www.census.gov and then OnTheMap for Emergency Management under Quick Links.

## Virtual USA (vUSA)

The Department of Homeland Security's Science and Technology Directorate's Command, Control, and Interoperability Division has launched Virtual USA (vUSA), an end-user driven and federally supported initiative focusing on cross-jurisdictional information sharing and collaboration among the homeland security and emergency management community.

VUSA links disparate tools and technologies in order to share the location and operational status of power and water lines, flood detectors, helicopter-capable landing sites, emergency vehicle and ambulance locations, weather and traffic conditions, evacuation routes, and school and government building floor plans across Federal, State, and local government, and does so without requiring any State to change either the system it now uses or the way it does business.

Information sharing starts at the local and State levels. Two examples of States that have made significant advances in developing State collaboration and information-sharing systems are Alabama and Virginia. With these new systems, these States have:

- Significantly increased their performance during emergency response.
- Saved time and money.
- Broken barriers to information among agencies, localities, and disciplines.

## Real-Time Volunteer Geographic Information (VGI) through Social Media and Open-Web Technologies

With the widespread use of smart phones and social media it has becoming very common for citizens to share information about an incident as it is happening. More and more frequently, volunteer geographic information (VGI) is being used to supplement formal communications and incident information when those resources may not be available, and also when the people affected by an incident can communicate location, pictures, and other information in real-time through their phones. VGI data have been effectively used by first responders to respond, locate victims, and save lives. Two key resources are available through VGI:

- **CrisisCommons** seeks to advance and support the use of open data and volunteer technology to catalyze innovation in crisis management and global development. CrisisCommons actively supports CrisisCamp, a barcamp event, which seeks to connect a global network of volunteers who use creative

problemsolving and open technologies to help people and communities in times and places of crisis.
- **Ushahidi** is a nonprofit software company that specializes in developing free and open source software for information collection, visualization, and interactive mapping.

## Lesson Summary

You have completed the Specialized GIS Tools and Off-the-Shelf Products lesson. This lesson described a number of resources that are available for specialized GIS use requirements.